THE ADVENTURES OF HENRY THE CITY CAT™

Freedom

by Debby Summers/illustrated by Eric Reese

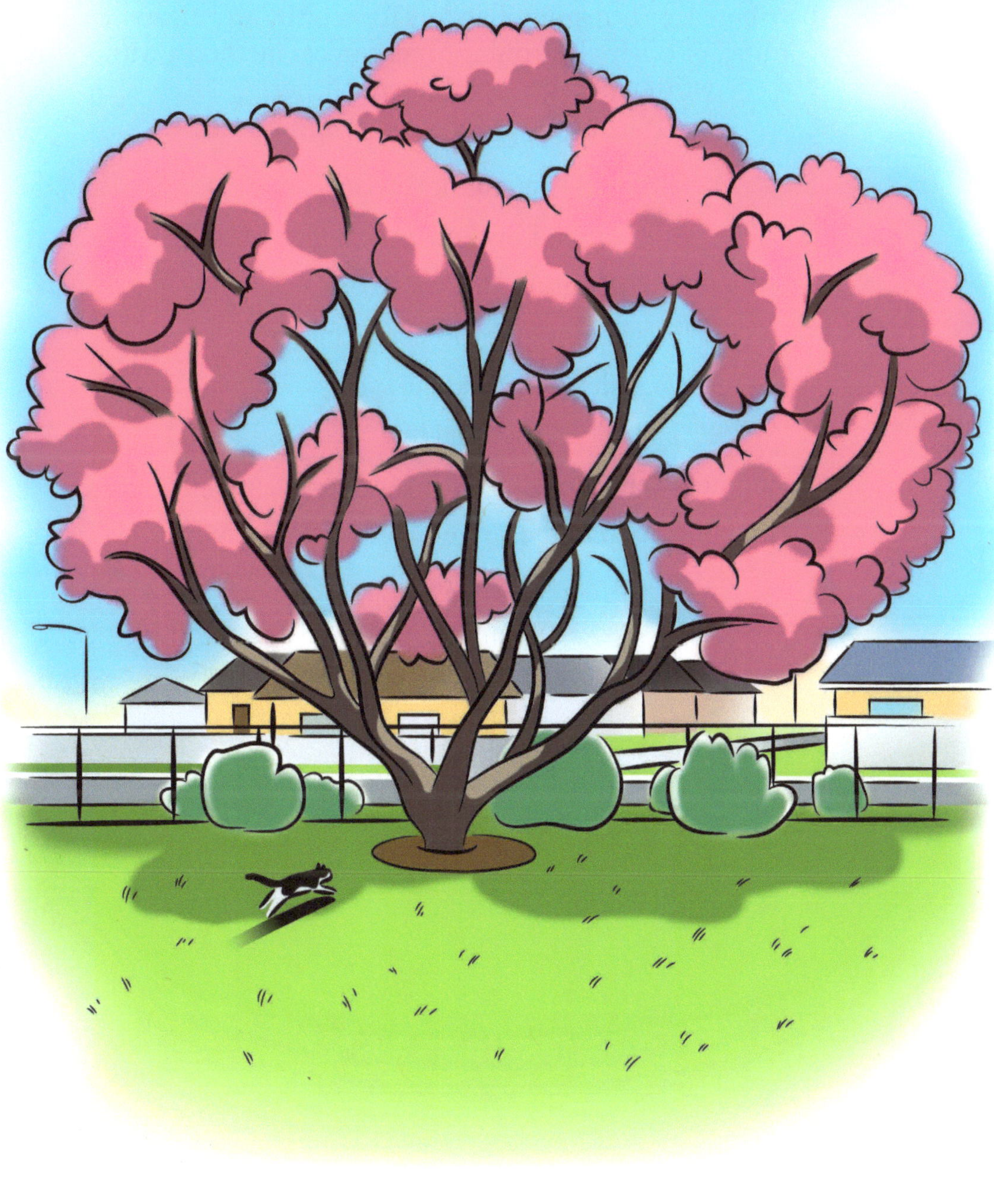

"The Adventures of Henry the City Cat"

"Freedom"

Copyright © 2017

Written by Debby Summers

All rights reserved.

No part of this publication to include illustrations, photographs or text may be used, reproduced, distributed, or transmitted in any form or by any means, including photocopying, recording, or other electronic or mechanical methods, without the prior written permission of the publisher.

"The Adventures of Henry the City Cat"

Title Trademark ™2016

Book Series Published by Summers Self-publishing

Illustrations by Eric Reese

Interior design by Rebecca Shaw

Alexandria, AL 36250

Distributed by

Summers Self-Publishing, Alexandria, AL 36250

Manufactured in the United States of America

1st Edition

Volume 2

ISBN:

ISBN-978-0-9983713-3-7

Table of Contents

Too Young 5

Mom's New Friend 7

Freedom 11

Orangey 19

Chloe 23

Chloe vs Orangey 29

Home At Last 31

Old Age 33

TOO YOUNG

It had been several months since Henry was first adopted and moved into the apartment.

Meredith was not ready to allow Henry to go outside on his own, except on the fenced and covered deck.

He cautiously watched the bats and swallows dive in flight for mosquitoes, as they flew swiftly through the air. At times, the swallows came onto the deck where Henry was crouched down in fear, but curiosity kept him watching through the wooden slats that fenced in the deck.

MOM'S NEW FRIEND

Meredith met and became friends with a coworker named Jason. Meredith invited Jason over to her apartment for a home-cooked meal. When Jason walked into the apartment, Henry ran and hid when he heard the deep, unfamiliar voice.

Meredith took Jason on a tour of her home to include the covered deck. When they came back inside, Jason caught a glimpse of Henry hiding in the corner of the hallway near one of the bedrooms.

Meredith reached down and picked up Henry as she walked towards Jason so the two could meet.

Meowing and squirming, Henry tried to get out of Meredith's arms because he wasn't interested in meeting mom's new friend. Once loose, Henry ran to the back bedroom where he could hide, but continue to keep an eye on Jason.

Jason came over to Meredith's home for dinner at least once a week. With each visit, Jason called out to

Henry to try and persuade him out of hiding to become friends. Eventually, Henry came out of hiding to visit with this tall stranger that made his mom laugh. Henry became comfortable enough with Jason to jump up in his lap for attention.

When Jason was a young man, he adopted two cats. He was used to them jumping up onto his lap and the amount of hair they shed onto clothing. Jason loved cats' independence. He told Meredith it is easier to leave them alone when going on short vacations because cats need only food, water and a litter box.

However, Jason lived where cats were not allowed in his apartment.

FREEDOM

Meredith and Jason fell in love and decided to marry. Because Meredith's apartment was too far from work, and Jason wasn't allowed to have pets in his apartment, they decided to buy a home.

Henry now lived in a big house with a fenced-in backyard that was much safer for young cats to explore and play outside. Henry hoped it would be just like it was at the apartment with cats running and playing, chasing butterflies, hunting mice and rats, jumping and climbing on old tree stumps, and on top of cars.

Henry hoped the cats in this new neighborhood would teach him all the things he saw cats do to have fun and survive in the jungle. But it wasn't like that at all in his new neighborhood.

Henry missed the view from the apartment window that he once had of the jungle. He missed watching cats chase butterflies and hunt the animals in the jungle.

Henry was almost one year old when mom finally let him go outside in the backyard. Henry was finally free to explore his new surroundings.

On one side of the backyard was the tallest, widest tree that Henry had ever seen. Mom called it a redbud tree. The tree limbs were long and tall.

Henry had never climbed a tree before, but he let his instincts kick in and without fear Henry climbed up high enough to see for a long distance beyond his neighborhood.

Instead of a jungle of trees, the neighborhood was a concrete jungle.

There were so many homes built side by side. As far as Henry could see, there were only a few trees, lots of roof tops, concrete driveways, and barking dogs.

Henry did not see cats from the view he had, but he saw and heard lots of dogs barking, and in every yard.

Henry remembered the day Mom came into his life. There were so many barking dogs in the kennels across from him.

Henry never wanted to live like that again!

At least there was freedom to run away from dogs in his new backyard.

Henry could jump over the chain link fence to explore his new neighborhood. He soon discovered there was no jungle around to play in, but there were large, scary barking dogs that lived on one side of his home and small, scary barking dogs that lived on the other side. Across the street were several homes without dogs.

Henry cautiously checked out that side of the street. He hoped to meet another cat that would teach him how to chase butterflies and hunt mice in the new neighborhood. It was a different environment than what Henry was used to seeing, and it frightened Henry.

He stayed close to home and spent most of his time in the backyard with the wire fence and the tall tree with long branches where he felt safe.

ORANGEY

Henry started to explore his new yard and jumped the fence to check out the front of the house. He crouched down by the garage door where he felt safe.

Suddenly, out of nowhere Henry saw a large, orange and white striped cat walking towards him. Her name was Orangey, and she lived across the street from Henry. After a few meows, Henry followed Orangey as she led him across the street to check out the new neighborhood. Every morning and every evening, Henry would lay on the windowsill hoping to see Orangey in the front yard.

She liked to sharpen her claws on the trunk of the large pear tree in Henry's front yard, as she waited patiently for Henry to join her for new adventures.

Orangey was an old cat and old cats teach kittens life lessons such as how to chase rats and mice, climb fences

to get a better look around or run fast to get away from big dogs. Henry meowed with excitement to see Orangey. He must have wondered what life lessons she would teach him today.

At last, Henry had a mentor who took him on adventures and she lived right across the street from Henry.

Orangey led Henry to check out the concrete jungle and the yards in this new neighborhood. Henry soon learned when it was safe to cross the street.

Henry discovered wooden privacy fences in the yards of some of the homes. Henry learned the faster that he ran, and the higher he could jump up on the tallest fence, the safer he would be in his travels through the concrete jungle.

From the height of the privacy fence, Henry could look down into each yard to see if there were dogs or other cats.

Thanks to Orangey's daily adventures and life lessons on how to survive in the concrete jungle, Henry quickly learned how to protect himself.

Henry also learned how to catch mice and rats just like the older cats. Henry was so proud of his new talent that he started leaving them on the door step, so Mom would be proud of him, also.

CHLOE

Before Henry had time to get used to his new home and the loud barking dogs that lived around him, Meredith brought home a large scary dog to live in the house with Henry. Meredith called her Chloe.

Chloe was an old Boxer breed dog with brown fur, a short tail, long ears, and she stood very tall next to Henry.

Although she was old, and slow to get around due to pain in her hips, Chloe still enjoyed investigating anything new, and that included Henry.

Chloe checked out each room in her new home sniffing every corner to make sure she did not miss anything that might tell her if another dog lived here before she moved in. They might have hidden a doggy treat to eat later because that is what some dogs do. Some dogs might not be hungry for a snack at the time their mom or dad gives it

to them, so they will hide the snack to eat later in the night, after their mom and dad have gone to bed.

Once Chloe had investigated the entire house corner to corner, room to room, it was time to check out this black and white, four-legged feline that Mom called Henry.

Chloe had not lived with cats before and was curious about Henry. She sniffed at Henry every time he walked by, and just to be a nuisance, followed Henry all over the house.

Chloe knew Henry was afraid of her, and used every opportunity to prove that in this home, she is head of the animal kingdom. Henry would show his teeth, hiss, and try scratching Chloe's nose as he meowed loudly for mom to save him. Chloe learned to fear those claws. Mom told Chloe to "lay down and leave Henry alone." Chloe knew she had to listen to Mom or she would have to stay outside. Chloe lay down to wait until Mom left the room. Chloe moved only her eyes from Mom back to Henry as if she was thinking, "This won't be the last time I scare Henry."

At the end of each long work day, Meredith would sit on the couch with a soft throw on her lap to fight the chill in the air. It became Henry's favorite place to take a nap and to find safety when Chloe was around.

In time, Chloe and Henry tolerated each other enough to stay in the same room together, but Chloe had better not get too close to Henry when he was laying in mom's lap or Chloe would get a slap with claws across her nose.

Henry left several scratches on Chloe's nose, as Henry was also protective of mom when Chloe came around.

When Henry scratched Chloe hard enough on her nose to draw blood, that was the last day Chloe teased Henry.

CHLOE VS ORANGEY

Chloe ran out the front door barking loudly when Meredith was letting Henry in. Chloe ran right into Orangey and came to a screeching stop. Orangey hissing and scratching at Chloe, began to back away to look at this old dog who was nothing but legs.

Orangey was not intimidated by Chloe's size and was ready to fight for the

space that she occupied. Chloe was very nervous and began to slowly walk backwards from this frightening orange and white cat. Chloe didn't have sharp claws like cats and couldn't fight back the way cats can, so Chloe backed up and ran back inside the house.

HOME AT LAST

Meredith and Jason decided to move to Alabama where Meredith could live close to her family. The community was quiet with very little traffic.

Behind Henry's new home was a heavily wooded cattle pasture separated by a chain link fence.

Because all the homes had big yards, there was space for Henry to live out the rest of his life with the largest jungle of trees right behind his house.

He no longer had to worry about crossing a street or dodging traffic to play in the jungle. The jungle was behind Henry's house, just beyond the chain link fence.

The many cats and kittens that lived in the subdivision visited Henry at night. Sometimes, Mom would put out food and water for them, just in case they were hungry or thirsty.

Henry had cats to play with and kittens to mentor. For Henry, this was a dream come true. It was the best place he ever lived or ever dreamt of living. It was a quiet community with lots of dogs and cats. But the dogs no longer frightened Henry. He found his inner strength, and he was a smart cat. After all, Henry survived the bats and swallows when they swooped down close to him on the covered deck where he first lived in the apartment. It seemed at times they were close enough to peck at Henry's fur, but they were hunting mosquitoes and too busy to notice him.

At the first sight of lizards and frogs, Henry thought they were scary looking, but he learned they only eat bugs. The scariest animal for Henry to survive were dogs of all sizes.

OLD AGE

Henry is an old cat now. He can't jump fences as high as he used to. Old age makes his body ache. Henry found part of the fence next to his neighbor was open wide enough that he could walk inside the backyard.

Mom worries that Henry may not be able to run fast enough to get away from dogs or bigger cats who like to fight. Mom won't let Henry stay out all night anymore. Henry has to come inside when she goes to bed.

The fenced-in backyard is very large with many tall trees for Henry to climb. Henry also enjoys scratching the tree bark to sharpen his claws.

Henry's favorite place to take a nap is in the middle of a flower garden filled with red rose bushes and yellow day lilies.

For the past few days, Meredith has noticed that Henry has not been feeling well (eating less, sleeping later than usual, and staying outside longer each day, but he always comes home at bedtime.)

One evening at bedtime, Meredith called for Henry to come inside. He was nowhere to be found. Jason came outside to help Meredith call for Henry. After calling repeatedly without any sign of Henry, Jason decided to get a flashlight and look around the big yard in case something might have happened to Henry and he was unable to walk. Jason shined the light in the direction of the backyard, the pasture and other areas where Henry often played. Meredith called for Henry once more and this time she heard dried leaves crunching under the weight of footsteps. The sounds grew louder and closer. Meredith grew excited and shouted out "Do you hear footsteps, Jason? It must be Henry and he heard our calls!" Jason said the sounds were too loud for a cat to make and thought it might be some other animal.

Jason shined the flashlight in the direction of the sounds and there was a large black and white cow with long horns walking along the back fence in the pasture. A meow was

heard coming from the direction of the cow. Jason shined his flashlight along the ground and walking alongside the cow and keeping up with the pace was Henry.

At first glance, it looked as if Henry was walking underneath this large beast, but at second glance, it was obvious, Henry was taking this cow on an adventure.

Meredith thought back to the time when Henry as a kitten sat on the couch meowing to go outside to play with the other cats. Who would have thought that almost 14 years later Henry would take a cow on a night stroll?

Henry wasn't just another cat, he was the King of the Jungle and even the largest beast in the jungle pasture traveled with him.

THE END.

www.ingramcontent.com/pod-product-compliance
Lightning Source LLC
Chambersburg PA
CBHW041125300426
44113CB00002B/64